THIS JOURNAL BELONGS TO:

_____

_____

Copyright© 2021 Faith Joy Solum

All rights reserved. No part of this publication may be reproduced, distributed, or transmitted in any form or by any means, including photocopying, recording, or other electronic or mechanical methods, without the prior written permission of the publisher, except in the case of brief quotations embodied in critical reviews and certain other noncommercial uses permitted by copyright law. For permission requests, write to the publisher, addressed "Attention: Permission Coordinator," via electronic correspondence at the website address below.

ISBN: 978-1-7375726-3-3 (Hardcover)
ISBN: 978-1-7375726-2-6 (Paperback)

Book design by: Faith Joy Solum
Cover art by: Jenna (Moss) Satterthwaite

Printed in the United States of America
Published by: Faith Joy Books

www.faithjoybooks.com

Welcome to The New You

This is no ordinary journal. This is a super-charged journal, packed with action steps and advice to help you move from feeling stuck to feeling unstoppable - all in 60 days.

Why 60 days?

Research has shown that it takes **66** days on average to make a new behavior automatic. That's an *average*. There's really no right or wrong timeline. If you follow the prompts in this journal **every day**, you will be well on your way to changing your thoughts and your life in two short months.

Don't stop there!

Once you are on your way, make sure you stay in motion by getting another *My High Five Journal* or looking at other journaling and goal setting options. The critical thing is that you **stay in motion** to reach your goals.

Here's a HIGH FIVE from me and let's get started.

Faith Joy Solum

What You Will Learn

You are going to learn to connect your body, mind, and spirit through breathing and positive thoughts.

Body

How to love and appreciate your body and all it does for you.

Mind

How to take control of your mind through mirror work and positive thoughts.

Spirit

How to connect with your joy by lowering your stress and getting in tune with what makes you happy.

We are holistic beings. What we do in one area of our lives affects everything else. This is why *My High Five Journal* takes a holistic approach to journaling. As you use this journal, you will gradually see your life improving in areas you may not have even thought about before. Sound exciting? It is!

TODAY'S DATE: /   /

Centered Breath

*First, **center your body** by sitting still, closing your eyes and breathing slowly and deeply for 15 breaths. Your lower ribs should expand with each inhale and contract with each exhale.*

My daily mantra is _____

_____

Today I love myself for _____

_____

Today I forgive myself for _____

_____

Today I promise myself that _____

_____

Looking in a mirror, make contact with your eyes and recite your four items from above. This is called mirror work.

Mirror work is an exercise in getting to know yourself. It increases your self-confidence, your inner peace, and develops a deeper sense of trust in yourself and in life.

Loving Mind

I am worthy of love because _____

_____

I accept all of me with love, including _____

_____

I deserve to be happy because _____

_____

What You Will Learn

You are going to learn to connect your body, mind, and spirit through breathing and positive thoughts.

Body

How to love and appreciate your body and all it does for you.

Mind

How to take control of your mind through mirror work and positive thoughts.

Spirit

How to connect with your joy by lowering your stress and getting in tune with what makes you happy.

We are holistic beings. What we do in one area of our lives affects everything else. This is why *My High Five Journal* takes a holistic approach to journaling. As you use this journal, you will gradually see your life improving in areas you may not have even thought about before. Sound exciting? It is!

TODAY'S DATE: /   /

Centered Breath

*First, **center your body** by sitting still, closing your eyes and breathing slowly and deeply for 15 breaths. Your lower ribs should expand with each inhale and contract with each exhale.*

My daily mantra is _____

_____

Today I love myself for _____

_____

Today I forgive myself for _____

_____

Today I promise myself that _____

_____

Looking in a mirror, make contact with your eyes and recite your four items from above. This is called mirror work.

Mirror work is an exercise in getting to know yourself. It increases your self-confidence, your inner peace, and develops a deeper sense of trust in yourself and in life.

Loving Mind

I am worthy of love because _____

_____

I accept all of me with love, including _____

_____

I deserve to be happy because _____

_____

TODAY'S DATE: ___ / ___ / ___

Grateful Spirit

List one person, one item (tangible or nontangible), and one personal attribute you are grateful for and why.

1) _____
   _____

2) _____
   _____

3) _____
   _____

Healthy Body

Being healthy is about showing love and respect for your body. Write your main health goal and one action you will do today to work towards that goal.

My main health goal is _____
_____

My action item today is _____
_____

Positive Outlook

What are three things you want at some point in your life? (Big, small, or in between.)

1) _____
2) _____
3) _____

grat·i·tude: the quality of being thankful; readiness to show appreciation for and to return kindness.

TODAY'S DATE: /   /

Centered Breath

*First, **center your body** by sitting still, closing your eyes and breathing slowly and deeply for 15 breaths. Your lower ribs should expand with each inhale and contract with each exhale.*

My daily mantra is _____

_____

Today I love myself for _____

_____

Today I forgive myself for _____

_____

Today I promise myself that _____

_____

Looking in a mirror, make contact with your eyes and recite your four items from above. This is called mirror work.

TIP: Make your mantra or goal rhyme and it will stick with you better. One example is, "I am feeling happy, light and alive at my perfect body weight of 155!" It should be meaningful to you.

Loving Mind

I am worthy of love because _____

_____

I accept all of me with love, including _____

_____

I deserve to be happy because _____

_____

TODAY'S DATE: /   /

Grateful Spirit

List one person, one item (tangible or nontangible), and one personal attribute you are grateful for and why.

1) _____

_____

2) _____

_____

3) _____

_____

Healthy Body

Being healthy is about showing love and respect for your body. Write your main health goal and one action you will do today to work towards that goal.

My main health goal is _____

_____

My action item today is _____

_____

Positive Outlook

What are three things you want at some point in your life? (Big, small, or in between.)

1) _____
2) _____
3) _____

Watch the way you talk to yourself. Instead of saying, "I'm an idiot" say, "It's okay, everyone makes mistakes."

TODAY'S DATE: /   /

Centered Breath

*First, **center your body** by sitting still, closing your eyes and breathing slowly and deeply for 15 breaths. Your lower ribs should expand with each inhale and contract with each exhale.*

My daily mantra is _____
_____

Today I love myself for _____
_____

Today I forgive myself for _____
_____

Today I promise myself that _____
_____

Looking in a mirror, make contact with your eyes and recite your four items from above. This is called mirror work.

You are probably going to miss a day of journaling here and there and that's okay. Even 2 days is okay, but if you miss 3 days, you just started a pattern. Never miss 3 days in a row.

Loving Mind

I am worthy of love because _____
_____

I accept all of me with love, including _____
_____

I deserve to be happy because _____
_____

TODAY'S DATE: /   /

Grateful Spirit

List one person, one item (tangible or nontangible), and one personal attribute you are grateful for and why.

1) _____

_____

2) _____

_____

3) _____

_____

Healthy Body

Being healthy is about showing love and respect for your body. Write your main health goal and one action you will do today to work towards that goal.

My main health goal is _____

_____

My action item today is _____

_____

Positive Outlook

What are three things you want at some point in your life? (Big, small, or in between.)

1) _____
2) _____
3) _____

Consistent, daily habits are the key to results.

TODAY'S DATE: /   /

Centered Breath

*First, **center your body** by sitting still, closing your eyes and breathing slowly and deeply for 15 breaths. Your lower ribs should expand with each inhale and contract with each exhale.*

My daily mantra is _____
_____

Today I love myself for _____
_____

Today I forgive myself for _____
_____

Today I promise myself that _____
_____

Looking in a mirror, make contact with your eyes and recite your four items from above. This is called mirror work.

4-4-4-4: When breathing, try inhaling through your nose for 4 seconds, holding the breath for 4 seconds, exhaling through the mouth for 4 seconds, and holding again for 4 seconds.

Loving Mind

I am worthy of love because _____
_____

I accept all of me with love, including _____
_____

I deserve to be happy because _____
_____

TODAY'S DATE: /   /

Grateful Spirit

List one person, one item (tangible or nontangible), and one personal attribute you are grateful for and why.

1) _____
   _____

2) _____
   _____

3) _____
   _____

Healthy Body

Being healthy is about showing love and respect for your body. Write your main health goal and one action you will do today to work towards that goal.

My main health goal is _____
_____

My action item today is _____
_____

Positive Outlook

What are three things you want at some point in your life? (Big, small, or in between.)

1) _____
2) _____
3) _____

Consistent, daily habits are the key to results.

TODAY'S DATE: /   /

Centered Breath

*First, **center your body** by sitting still, closing your eyes and breathing slowly and deeply for 15 breaths. Your lower ribs should expand with each inhale and contract with each exhale.*

My daily mantra is _____

_____

Today I love myself for _____

_____

Today I forgive myself for _____

_____

Today I promise myself that _____

_____

Looking in a mirror, make contact with your eyes and recite your four items from above. This is called mirror work.

4-4-4-4: When breathing, try inhaling through your nose for 4 seconds, holding the breath for 4 seconds, exhaling through the mouth for 4 seconds, and holding again for 4 seconds.

Loving Mind

I am worthy of love because _____

_____

I accept all of me with love, including _____

_____

I deserve to be happy because _____

_____

TODAY'S DATE: /   /

Grateful Spirit

List one person, one item (tangible or nontangible), and one personal attribute you are grateful for and why.

1) _____
   _____

2) _____
   _____

3) _____
   _____

Healthy Body

Being healthy is about showing love and respect for your body. Write your main health goal and one action you will do today to work towards that goal.

My main health goal is _____
_____

My action item today is _____
_____

Positive Outlook

What are three things you want at some point in your life? (Big, small, or in between.)

1) _____
2) _____
3) _____

Why NOT tell yourself how amazing, courageous, and confident you are? Start today. Make it a habit.

TODAY'S DATE: /   /

Centered Breath

*First, **center your body** by sitting still, closing your eyes and breathing slowly and deeply for 15 breaths. Your lower ribs should expand with each inhale and contract with each exhale.*

My daily mantra is _____

_____

Today I love myself for _____

_____

Today I forgive myself for _____

_____

Today I promise myself that _____

_____

Looking in a mirror, make contact with your eyes and recite your four items from above. This is called mirror work.

Change the way you look at things
and the things you look at change.
~Wayne Dyer~

Loving Mind

I am worthy of love because _____

_____

I accept all of me with love, including _____

_____

I deserve to be happy because _____

_____

TODAY'S DATE: ___ / ___ / ___

Grateful Spirit

List one person, one item (tangible or nontangible), and one personal attribute you are grateful for and why.

1) _____
_____

2) _____
_____

3) _____
_____

Healthy Body

Being healthy is about showing love and respect for your body. Write your main health goal and one action you will do today to work towards that goal.

My main health goal is _____
_____

My action item today is _____
_____

Positive Outlook

What are three things you want at some point in your life? (Big, small, or in between.)

1) _____
2) _____
3) _____

You can write the same three things you want every day. The more you write them, the stronger the desire.

TODAY'S DATE: /   /

Centered Breath

*First, **center your body** by sitting still, closing your eyes and breathing slowly and deeply for 15 breaths. Your lower ribs should expand with each inhale and contract with each exhale.*

My daily mantra is _____

_____

Today I love myself for _____

_____

Today I forgive myself for _____

_____

Today I promise myself that _____

_____

Looking in a mirror, make contact with your eyes and recite your four items from above. This is called mirror work.

Gratitude has many health benefits, including improving sleep, resilience, and self-esteem while reducing stress, anxiety, and depression. **Practice gratitude daily** and enjoy the rewards!

Loving Mind

I am worthy of love because _____

_____

I accept all of me with love, including _____

_____

I deserve to be happy because _____

_____

TODAY'S DATE: ___ / ___ / ___

Grateful Spirit

List one person, one item (tangible or nontangible), and one personal attribute you are grateful for and why.

1) _____
   _____

2) _____
   _____

3) _____
   _____

Healthy Body

Being healthy is about showing love and respect for your body. Write your main health goal and one action you will do today to work towards that goal.

My main health goal is _____
_____

My action item today is _____
_____

Positive Outlook

What are three things you want at some point in your life? (Big, small, or in between.)

1) _____
2) _____
3) _____

What you focus on expands, so be sure you are focusing on what you want to attract into your life.

TODAY'S DATE: /   /

Centered Breath

*First, **center your body** by sitting still, closing your eyes and breathing slowly and deeply for 15 breaths. Your lower ribs should expand with each inhale and contract with each exhale.*

My daily mantra is _____

_____

Today I love myself for _____

_____

Today I forgive myself for _____

_____

Today I promise myself that _____

_____

Looking in a mirror, make contact with your eyes and recite your four items from above. This is called mirror work.

Move your body today! Exercise improves memory and brain function, lowers blood pressure, improves sleep, reduces anxiety, combats cancer-related fatigue, and so much more!

Loving Mind

I am worthy of love because _____

_____

I accept all of me with love, including _____

_____

I deserve to be happy because _____

_____

TODAY'S DATE: ___ / ___ / ___

Grateful Spirit

List one person, one item (tangible or nontangible), and one personal attribute you are grateful for and why.

1) _____
_____

2) _____
_____

3) _____
_____

Healthy Body

Being healthy is about showing love and respect for your body. Write your main health goal and one action you will do today to work towards that goal.

My main health goal is _____
_____

My action item today is _____
_____

Positive Outlook

What are three things you want at some point in your life? (Big, small, or in between.)

1) _____
2) _____
3) _____

What you focus on expands, so be sure you are focusing on what you want to attract into your life.

TODAY'S DATE: ___ / ___ / ___

Centered Breath

*First, **center your body** by sitting still, closing your eyes and breathing slowly and deeply for 15 breaths. Your lower ribs should expand with each inhale and contract with each exhale.*

My daily mantra is _____
_____

Today I love myself for _____
_____

Today I forgive myself for _____
_____

Today I promise myself that _____
_____

Looking in a mirror, make contact with your eyes and recite your four items from above. This is called mirror work.

Move your body today! Exercise improves memory and brain function, lowers blood pressure, improves sleep, reduces anxiety, combats cancer-related fatigue, and so much more!

Loving Mind

I am worthy of love because _____
_____

I accept all of me with love, including _____
_____

I deserve to be happy because _____
_____

TODAY'S DATE: ___ / ___ / ___

Grateful Spirit

List one person, one item (tangible or nontangible), and one personal attribute you are grateful for and why.

1) _____
   _____

2) _____
   _____

3) _____
   _____

Healthy Body

Being healthy is about showing love and respect for your body. Write your main health goal and one action you will do today to work towards that goal.

My main health goal is _____
_____

My action item today is _____
_____

Positive Outlook

What are three things you want at some point in your life? (Big, small, or in between.)

1) _____
2) _____
3) _____

Be real with how you feel. Your feelings are valid and they don't make you broken or weak.

TODAY'S DATE: /   /

Centered Breath

*First, **center your body** by sitting still, closing your eyes and breathing slowly and deeply for 15 breaths. Your lower ribs should expand with each inhale and contract with each exhale.*

My daily mantra is _____

_____

Today I love myself for _____

_____

Today I forgive myself for _____

_____

Today I promise myself that _____

_____

Looking in a mirror, make contact with your eyes and recite your four items from above. This is called mirror work.

You are enough.
You have always been enough.
You will always be enough.

Loving Mind

I am worthy of love because _____

_____

I accept all of me with love, including _____

_____

I deserve to be happy because _____

_____

TODAY'S DATE: /   /

Grateful Spirit

List one person, one item (tangible or nontangible), and one personal attribute you are grateful for and why.

1) _____

   _____

2) _____

   _____

3) _____

   _____

Healthy Body

Being healthy is about showing love and respect for your body. Write your main health goal and one action you will do today to work towards that goal.

My main health goal is _____

_____

My action item today is _____

_____

Positive Outlook

What are three things you want at some point in your life? (Big, small, or in between.)

1) _____
2) _____
3) _____

Today, you will make great decisions because you will make them with concious awareness.

TODAY'S DATE: /   /

Centered Breath

*First, **center your body** by sitting still, closing your eyes and breathing slowly and deeply for 15 breaths. Your lower ribs should expand with each inhale and contract with each exhale.*

My daily mantra is _____

_____

Today I love myself for _____

_____

Today I forgive myself for _____

_____

Today I promise myself that _____

_____

Looking in a mirror, make contact with your eyes and recite your four items from above. This is called mirror work.

Mindfulness is being consciously aware and focused on the present moment while calmly accepting and acknowledging your thoughts, emotions and bodily sensations.

Loving Mind

I am worthy of love because _____

_____

I accept all of me with love, including _____

_____

I deserve to be happy because _____

_____

TODAY'S DATE: ____ / ____ / ____

Grateful Spirit

List one person, one item (tangible or nontangible), and one personal attribute you are grateful for and why.

1) _____
_____

2) _____
_____

3) _____
_____

Healthy Body

Being healthy is about showing love and respect for your body. Write your main health goal and one action you will do today to work towards that goal.

My main health goal is _____
_____

My action item today is _____
_____

Positive Outlook

What are three things you want at some point in your life? (Big, small, or in between.)

1) _____
2) _____
3) _____

Do something today to make yourself laugh hard.
REALLY HARD!

TODAY'S DATE: ___ / ___ / ___

Centered Breath

*First, **center your body** by sitting still, closing your eyes and breathing slowly and deeply for 15 breaths. Your lower ribs should expand with each inhale and contract with each exhale.*

My daily mantra is _____

_____

Today I love myself for _____

_____

Today I forgive myself for _____

_____

Today I promise myself that _____

_____

Looking in a mirror, make contact with your eyes and recite your four items from above. This is called mirror work.

Try this mantra:
Right now, in this moment, I am safe,
I am loved, I am enough.

Loving Mind

I am worthy of love because _____

_____

I accept all of me with love, including _____

_____

I deserve to be happy because _____

_____

TODAY'S DATE: /   /

Grateful Spirit

List one person, one item (tangible or nontangible), and one personal attribute you are grateful for and why.

1) _____
_____

2) _____
_____

3) _____
_____

Healthy Body

Being healthy is about showing love and respect for your body. Write your main health goal and one action you will do today to work towards that goal.

My main health goal is _____
_____

My action item today is _____
_____

Positive Outlook

What are three things you want at some point in your life? (Big, small, or in between.)

1) _____
2) _____
3) _____

There is comfort in knowing that if we don't like how a previous choice turned out, we can choose again.

TODAY'S DATE: /   /

Centered Breath

*First, **center your body** by sitting still, closing your eyes and breathing slowly and deeply for 15 breaths. Your lower ribs should expand with each inhale and contract with each exhale.*

My daily mantra is _____
_____

Today I love myself for _____
_____

Today I forgive myself for _____
_____

Today I promise myself that _____
_____

Looking in a mirror, make contact with your eyes and recite your four items from above. This is called mirror work.

Give what you want to receive.
It is a universal law that you do not get what you want, you get what you give.

Loving Mind

I am worthy of love because _____
_____

I accept all of me with love, including _____
_____

I deserve to be happy because _____
_____

TODAY'S DATE: ____ / ____ / ____

Grateful Spirit

List one person, one item (tangible or nontangible), and one personal attribute you are grateful for and why.

1) _____

_____

2) _____

_____

3) _____

_____

Healthy Body

Being healthy is about showing love and respect for your body. Write your main health goal and one action you will do today to work towards that goal.

My main health goal is _____

_____

My action item today is _____

_____

Positive Outlook

What are three things you want at some point in your life? (Big, small, or in between.)

1) _____
2) _____
3) _____

Perform a secret act of kindness today and pay attention to how you feel after.

TODAY'S DATE: /   /

Centered Breath

*First, **center your body** by sitting still, closing your eyes and breathing slowly and deeply for 15 breaths. Your lower ribs should expand with each inhale and contract with each exhale.*

My daily mantra is _____

_____

Today I love myself for _____

_____

Today I forgive myself for _____

_____

Today I promise myself that _____

_____

Looking in a mirror, make contact with your eyes and recite your four items from above. This is called mirror work.

*Not every **beautiful moment** can be captured in a picture.
Most are captured in your heart.
That is what your heart is for.*

Loving Mind

I am worthy of love because _____

_____

I accept all of me with love, including _____

_____

I deserve to be happy because _____

_____

TODAY'S DATE: ____ / ____ / ____

Grateful Spirit

List one person, one item (tangible or nontangible), and one personal attribute you are grateful for and why.

1) _____
_____

2) _____
_____

3) _____
_____

Healthy Body

Being healthy is about showing love and respect for your body. Write your main health goal and one action you will do today to work towards that goal.

My main health goal is _____
_____

My action item today is _____
_____

Positive Outlook

What are three things you want at some point in your life? (Big, small, or in between.)

1) _____
2) _____
3) _____

Challenges are opportunities hidden from those who are not willing to look for them.

TODAY'S DATE: /   /

Centered Breath

*First, **center your body** by sitting still, closing your eyes and breathing slowly and deeply for 15 breaths. Your lower ribs should expand with each inhale and contract with each exhale.*

My daily mantra is _____
_____

Today I love myself for _____
_____

Today I forgive myself for _____
_____

Today I promise myself that _____
_____

Looking in a mirror, make contact with your eyes and recite your four items from above. This is called mirror work.

Sleep is our protective state. It is where we heal, restore, rejuvenate, and gain spiritual alignment. It is also where we can reprogram our subconscious mind.

Loving Mind

I am worthy of love because _____
_____

I accept all of me with love, including _____
_____

I deserve to be happy because _____
_____

TODAY'S DATE: /   /

Grateful Spirit

List one person, one item (tangible or nontangible), and one personal attribute you are grateful for and why.

1) _____
_____

2) _____
_____

3) _____
_____

Healthy Body

Being healthy is about showing love and respect for your body. Write your main health goal and one action you will do today to work towards that goal.

My main health goal is _____
_____

My action item today is _____
_____

Positive Outlook

What are three things you want at some point in your life? (Big, small, or in between.)

1) _____
2) _____
3) _____

Choose your rut carefully, you'll be in it for a while.

TODAY'S DATE: /   /

Centered Breath

*First, **center your body** by sitting still, closing your eyes and breathing slowly and deeply for 15 breaths. Your lower ribs should expand with each inhale and contract with each exhale.*

My daily mantra is _____

_____

Today I love myself for _____

_____

Today I forgive myself for _____

_____

Today I promise myself that _____

_____

Looking in a mirror, make contact with your eyes and recite your four items from above. This is called mirror work.

Say this out loud at least 50 times today:
"I feel healthy! I feel happy! I feel terrific!"
Then, pay attention to how you feel throughout the day.

Loving Mind

I am worthy of love because _____

_____

I accept all of me with love, including _____

_____

I deserve to be happy because _____

_____

TODAY'S DATE: ___ / ___ / ___

Grateful Spirit

List one person, one item (tangible or nontangible), and one personal attribute you are grateful for and why.

1) _____

_____

2) _____

_____

3) _____

_____

Healthy Body

Being healthy is about showing love and respect for your body. Write your main health goal and one action you will do today to work towards that goal.

My main health goal is _____

_____

My action item today is _____

_____

Positive Outlook

What are three things you want at some point in your life? (Big, small, or in between.)

1) _____
2) _____
3) _____

Anything worth having is worth working for.
What are you willing to do for your dreams?

TODAY'S DATE: ___ / ___ / ___

Centered Breath

*First, **center your body** by sitting still, closing your eyes and breathing slowly and deeply for 15 breaths. Your lower ribs should expand with each inhale and contract with each exhale.*

My daily mantra is _____
_____

Today I love myself for _____
_____

Today I forgive myself for _____
_____

Today I promise myself that _____
_____

Looking in a mirror, make contact with your eyes and recite your four items from above. This is called mirror work.

Keep your mind focused on your morals and goals,
with faith that you will achieve,
and success will inevitably follow.

Loving Mind

I am worthy of love because _____
_____

I accept all of me with love, including _____
_____

I deserve to be happy because _____
_____

TODAY'S DATE: ____ / ____ / ____

Grateful Spirit

List one person, one item (tangible or nontangible), and one personal attribute you are grateful for and why.

1) _____

_____

2) _____

_____

3) _____

_____

Healthy Body

Being healthy is about showing love and respect for your body. Write your main health goal and one action you will do today to work towards that goal.

My main health goal is _____

_____

My action item today is _____

_____

Positive Outlook

What are three things you want at some point in your life? (Big, small, or in between.)

1) _____
2) _____
3) _____

What will you do with your power today?
What will you do with the power of you?

TODAY'S DATE: /   /

Centered Breath

*First, **center your body** by sitting still, closing your eyes and breathing slowly and deeply for 15 breaths. Your lower ribs should expand with each inhale and contract with each exhale.*

My daily mantra is _____
_____

Today I love myself for _____
_____

Today I forgive myself for _____
_____

Today I promise myself that _____
_____

Looking in a mirror, make contact with your eyes and recite your four items from above. This is called mirror work.

Rise above negativity. Train yourself to dismiss doubt and disbelief. It doesn't just happen. It takes time and practice to make positivity and optimism a habit.

Loving Mind

I am worthy of love because _____
_____

I accept all of me with love, including _____
_____

I deserve to be happy because _____
_____

TODAY'S DATE: /   /

Grateful Spirit

List one person, one item (tangible or nontangible), and one personal attribute you are grateful for and why.

1) _____

_____

2) _____

_____

3) _____

_____

Healthy Body

Being healthy is about showing love and respect for your body. Write your main health goal and one action you will do today to work towards that goal.

My main health goal is _____

_____

My action item today is _____

_____

Positive Outlook

What are three things you want at some point in your life? (Big, small, or in between.)

1) _____
2) _____
3) _____

Take action on one positive thought today!

TODAY'S DATE: /   /

Centered Breath

*First, **center your body** by sitting still, closing your eyes and breathing slowly and deeply for 15 breaths. Your lower ribs should expand with each inhale and contract with each exhale.*

My daily mantra is _____
_____

Today I love myself for _____
_____

Today I forgive myself for _____
_____

Today I promise myself that _____
_____

Looking in a mirror, make contact with your eyes and recite your four items from above. This is called mirror work.

Have you accepted your surroundings as a misfortune you will never overcome? If so, it's time to make a shift from practicing negative daily thoughts to practicing positive ones.

Loving Mind

I am worthy of love because _____
_____

I accept all of me with love, including _____
_____

I deserve to be happy because _____
_____

TODAY'S DATE: / /

Grateful Spirit

List one person, one item (tangible or nontangible), and one personal attribute you are grateful for and why.

1) _____

_____

2) _____

_____

3) _____

_____

Healthy Body

Being healthy is about showing love and respect for your body. Write your main health goal and one action you will do today to work towards that goal.

My main health goal is _____

_____

My action item today is _____

_____

Positive Outlook

What are three things you want at some point in your life? (Big, small, or in between.)

1) _____
2) _____
3) _____

Self love and acceptance is the only road to lasting change.

TODAY'S DATE: ____ / ____ / ____

Centered Breath

*First, **center your body** by sitting still, closing your eyes and breathing slowly and deeply for 15 breaths. Your lower ribs should expand with each inhale and contract with each exhale.*

My daily mantra is _____
_____

Today I love myself for _____
_____

Today I forgive myself for _____
_____

Today I promise myself that _____
_____

Looking in a mirror, make contact with your eyes and recite your four items from above. This is called mirror work.

Attachments to assumptions or beliefs can lead to self-shame. Truth in who you are leads to letting go of attachments and setting you free from their oppressing bonds.

Loving Mind

I am worthy of love because _____
_____

I accept all of me with love, including _____
_____

I deserve to be happy because _____
_____

TODAY'S DATE: ____ / ____ / ____

Grateful Spirit

List one person, one item (tangible or nontangible), and one personal attribute you are grateful for and why.

1) _____
   _____

2) _____
   _____

3) _____
   _____

Healthy Body

Being healthy is about showing love and respect for your body. Write your main health goal and one action you will do today to work towards that goal.

My main health goal is _____
_____

My action item today is _____
_____

Positive Outlook

What are three things you want at some point in your life? (Big, small, or in between.)

1) _____
2) _____
3) _____

A person shamed into making changes is not really changing anything.

TODAY'S DATE: /   /

Centered Breath

*First, **center your body** by sitting still, closing your eyes and breathing slowly and deeply for 15 breaths. Your lower ribs should expand with each inhale and contract with each exhale.*

My daily mantra is _____
_____

Today I love myself for _____
_____

Today I forgive myself for _____
_____

Today I promise myself that _____
_____

Looking in a mirror, make contact with your eyes and recite your four items from above. This is called mirror work.

Television and social media can contribute to negative thinking. Make a commitment to go without television and social media for today. If that's too easy, make it a week!

Loving Mind

I am worthy of love because _____
_____

I accept all of me with love, including _____
_____

I deserve to be happy because _____
_____

TODAY'S DATE: ___ / ___ / ___

Grateful Spirit

List one person, one item (tangible or nontangible), and one personal attribute you are grateful for and why.

1) _____
_____

2) _____
_____

3) _____
_____

Healthy Body

Being healthy is about showing love and respect for your body. Write your main health goal and one action you will do today to work towards that goal.

My main health goal is _____
_____

My action item today is _____
_____

Positive Outlook

What are three things you want at some point in your life? (Big, small, or in between.)

1) _____
2) _____
3) _____

All we have and all we are is love.

TODAY'S DATE: ____ / ____ / ____

Centered Breath

*First, **center your body** by sitting still, closing your eyes and breathing slowly and deeply for 15 breaths. Your lower ribs should expand with each inhale and contract with each exhale.*

My daily mantra is _____

_____

Today I love myself for _____

_____

Today I forgive myself for _____

_____

Today I promise myself that _____

_____

Looking in a mirror, make contact with your eyes and recite your four items from above. This is called mirror work.

Reasonable time is enough time to achieve all your goals. It's not the hours you put in, it's what you put in the hours.
~Jim Rohn~

Loving Mind

I am worthy of love because _____

_____

I accept all of me with love, including _____

_____

I deserve to be happy because _____

_____

TODAY'S DATE: ___/___/___

Grateful Spirit

List one person, one item (tangible or nontangible), and one personal attribute you are grateful for and why.

1) _____

_____

2) _____

_____

3) _____

_____

Healthy Body

Being healthy is about showing love and respect for your body. Write your main health goal and one action you will do today to work towards that goal.

My main health goal is _____

_____

My action item today is _____

_____

Positive Outlook

What are three things you want at some point in your life? (Big, small, or in between.)

1) _____
2) _____
3) _____

All we have and all we are is love.

TODAY'S DATE: /   /

Centered Breath

*First, **center your body** by sitting still, closing your eyes and breathing slowly and deeply for 15 breaths. Your lower ribs should expand with each inhale and contract with each exhale.*

My daily mantra is _____

_____

Today I love myself for _____

_____

Today I forgive myself for _____

_____

Today I promise myself that _____

_____

Looking in a mirror, make contact with your eyes and recite your four items from above. This is called mirror work.

Reasonable time is enough time to achieve all your goals. It's not the hours you put in, it's what you put in the hours.
~Jim Rohn~

Loving Mind

I am worthy of love because _____

_____

I accept all of me with love, including _____

_____

I deserve to be happy because _____

_____

TODAY'S DATE: / /

Grateful Spirit

List one person, one item (tangible or nontangible), and one personal attribute you are grateful for and why.

1) _____

_____

2) _____

_____

3) _____

_____

Healthy Body

Being healthy is about showing love and respect for your body. Write your main health goal and one action you will do today to work towards that goal.

My main health goal is _____

_____

My action item today is _____

_____

Positive Outlook

What are three things you want at some point in your life? (Big, small, or in between.)

1) _____
2) _____
3) _____

Be happy with what you have
while pursuing what you want.

TODAY'S DATE: ___ / ___ / ___

Centered Breath

*First, **center your body** by sitting still, closing your eyes and breathing slowly and deeply for 15 breaths. Your lower ribs should expand with each inhale and contract with each exhale.*

My daily mantra is _____

_____

Today I love myself for _____

_____

Today I forgive myself for _____

_____

Today I promise myself that _____

_____

Looking in a mirror, make contact with your eyes and recite your four items from above. This is called mirror work.

Complaining and gossiping are poison to your soul. Commit to stop your complaining and gossiping, and remove yourself from those around you who do.

Loving Mind

I am worthy of love because _____

_____

I accept all of me with love, including _____

_____

I deserve to be happy because _____

_____

TODAY'S DATE: ___ / ___ / ___

Grateful Spirit

List one person, one item (tangible or nontangible), and one personal attribute you are grateful for and why.

1) _____

_____

2) _____

_____

3) _____

_____

Healthy Body

Being healthy is about showing love and respect for your body. Write your main health goal and one action you will do today to work towards that goal.

My main health goal is _____

_____

My action item today is _____

_____

Positive Outlook

What are three things you want at some point in your life? (Big, small, or in between.)

1) _____
2) _____
3) _____

We see what we want to see and believe what we want to believe.

TODAY'S DATE: /   /

Centered Breath

*First, **center your body** by sitting still, closing your eyes and breathing slowly and deeply for 15 breaths. Your lower ribs should expand with each inhale and contract with each exhale.*

My daily mantra is _____
_____

Today I love myself for _____
_____

Today I forgive myself for _____
_____

Today I promise myself that _____
_____

Looking in a mirror, make contact with your eyes and recite your four items from above. This is called mirror work.

If you only ever did the things you don't want to do, you'd have everything you've ever wanted.
~Mel Robbins~

Loving Mind

I am worthy of love because _____
_____

I accept all of me with love, including _____
_____

I deserve to be happy because _____
_____

TODAY'S DATE: ___ / ___ / ___

Grateful Spirit

List one person, one item (tangible or nontangible), and one personal attribute you are grateful for and why.

1) _____
_____

2) _____
_____

3) _____
_____

Healthy Body

Being healthy is about showing love and respect for your body. Write your main health goal and one action you will do today to work towards that goal.

My main health goal is _____
_____

My action item today is _____
_____

Positive Outlook

What are three things you want at some point in your life? (Big, small, or in between.)

1) _____
2) _____
3) _____

Goals create the roadmap to your future life.

TODAY'S DATE: /   /

Centered Breath

*First, **center your body** by sitting still, closing your eyes and breathing slowly and deeply for 15 breaths. Your lower ribs should expand with each inhale and contract with each exhale.*

My daily mantra is _____

_____

Today I love myself for _____

_____

Today I forgive myself for _____

_____

Today I promise myself that _____

_____

Looking in a mirror, make contact with your eyes and recite your four items from above. This is called mirror work.

Fire Breathing: Sitting crosslegged on the floor, with hands on knees, inhale through your nose, expanding your belly, and immediately exhale forcefully. Continue rapidly for 30 seconds.

Loving Mind

I am worthy of love because _____

_____

I accept all of me with love, including _____

_____

I deserve to be happy because _____

_____

TODAY'S DATE: ____ / ____ / ____

Grateful Spirit

List one person, one item (tangible or nontangible), and one personal attribute you are grateful for and why.

1) _____
_____

2) _____
_____

3) _____
_____

Healthy Body

Being healthy is about showing love and respect for your body. Write your main health goal and one action you will do today to work towards that goal.

My main health goal is _____
_____

My action item today is _____
_____

Positive Outlook

What are three things you want at some point in your life? (Big, small, or in between.)

1) _____
2) _____
3) _____

It takes work to improve, which is why many people remain the same.

TODAY'S DATE: ____ / ____ / ____

Centered Breath

*First, **center your body** by sitting still, closing your eyes and breathing slowly and deeply for 15 breaths. Your lower ribs should expand with each inhale and contract with each exhale.*

My daily mantra is _____

_____

Today I love myself for _____

_____

Today I forgive myself for _____

_____

Today I promise myself that _____

_____

Looking in a mirror, make contact with your eyes and recite your four items from above. This is called mirror work.

Fill your life with more of what you love - more time with the people you love, more time doing the things you love. Start with just 5 minutes a day and notice the difference.

Loving Mind

I am worthy of love because _____

_____

I accept all of me with love, including _____

_____

I deserve to be happy because _____

_____

TODAY'S DATE: ___ / ___ / ___

Grateful Spirit

List one person, one item (tangible or nontangible), and one personal attribute you are grateful for and why.

1) _____
_____

2) _____
_____

3) _____
_____

Healthy Body

Being healthy is about showing love and respect for your body. Write your main health goal and one action you will do today to work towards that goal.

My main health goal is _____
_____

My action item today is _____
_____

Positive Outlook

What are three things you want at some point in your life? (Big, small, or in between.)

1) _____
2) _____
3) _____

Cultivate the garden of your character, seeds of great potential lie dormant there.

TODAY'S DATE: /   /

Centered Breath

*First, **center your body** by sitting still, closing your eyes and breathing slowly and deeply for 15 breaths. Your lower ribs should expand with each inhale and contract with each exhale.*

My daily mantra is _____
_____

Today I love myself for _____
_____

Today I forgive myself for _____
_____

Today I promise myself that _____
_____

Looking in a mirror, make contact with your eyes and recite your four items from above. This is called mirror work.

When **setting goals**, they should be appropriate, attainable, measurable, clearly stated, and require you to stretch a little. Once you make a goal, **write it down**, or it's merely a wish.

Loving Mind

I am worthy of love because _____
_____

I accept all of me with love, including _____
_____

I deserve to be happy because _____
_____

TODAY'S DATE: ___ / ___ / ___

Grateful Spirit

List one person, one item (tangible or nontangible), and one personal attribute you are grateful for and why.

1) _____
_____

2) _____
_____

3) _____
_____

Healthy Body

Being healthy is about showing love and respect for your body. Write your main health goal and one action you will do today to work towards that goal.

My main health goal is _____
_____

My action item today is _____
_____

Positive Outlook

What are three things you want at some point in your life? (Big, small, or in between.)

1) _____
2) _____
3) _____

A committed person cannot be kept from reaching success.

TODAY'S DATE: ___ / ___ / ___

Centered Breath

*First, **center your body** by sitting still, closing your eyes and breathing slowly and deeply for 15 breaths. Your lower ribs should expand with each inhale and contract with each exhale.*

My daily mantra is _____
_____

Today I love myself for _____
_____

Today I forgive myself for _____
_____

Today I promise myself that _____
_____

Looking in a mirror, make contact with your eyes and recite your four items from above. This is called mirror work.

Yoga is a great way to relieve stress because it incorporates breathing, stretching, and exercise. Practice with someone you enjoy being around, for additional stress relief benefits.

Loving Mind

I am worthy of love because _____
_____

I accept all of me with love, including _____
_____

I deserve to be happy because _____
_____

TODAY'S DATE: ____ / ____ / ____

Grateful Spirit

List one person, one item (tangible or nontangible), and one personal attribute you are grateful for and why.

1) _____

_____

2) _____

_____

3) _____

_____

Healthy Body

Being healthy is about showing love and respect for your body. Write your main health goal and one action you will do today to work towards that goal.

My main health goal is _____

_____

My action item today is _____

_____

Positive Outlook

What are three things you want at some point in your life? (Big, small, or in between.)

1) _____
2) _____
3) _____

Love your body and all that it does for you. Treat it with respect and kindness and it will flourish.

TODAY'S DATE: ___ / ___ / ___

Centered Breath

*First, **center your body** by sitting still, closing your eyes and breathing slowly and deeply for 15 breaths. Your lower ribs should expand with each inhale and contract with each exhale.*

My daily mantra is _____

_____

Today I love myself for _____

_____

Today I forgive myself for _____

_____

Today I promise myself that _____

_____

Looking in a mirror, make contact with your eyes and recite your four items from above. This is called mirror work.

The first step to improving your life is accepting where you are, right now. Today, look at your life and see it for what it is, not worse than what it is. Choose one thing to improve on.

Loving Mind

I am worthy of love because _____

_____

I accept all of me with love, including _____

_____

I deserve to be happy because _____

_____

TODAY'S DATE: /   /

Grateful Spirit

List one person, one item (tangible or nontangible), and one personal attribute you are grateful for and why.

1) _____

_____

2) _____

_____

3) _____

_____

Healthy Body

Being healthy is about showing love and respect for your body. Write your main health goal and one action you will do today to work towards that goal.

My main health goal is _____

_____

My action item today is _____

_____

Positive Outlook

What are three things you want at some point in your life? (Big, small, or in between.)

1) _____
2) _____
3) _____

You have to know where you are before you can navigate to someplace else.

TODAY'S DATE: /   /

Centered Breath

*First, **center your body** by sitting still, closing your eyes and breathing slowly and deeply for 15 breaths. Your lower ribs should expand with each inhale and contract with each exhale.*

My daily mantra is _____

_____

Today I love myself for _____

_____

Today I forgive myself for _____

_____

Today I promise myself that _____

_____

Looking in a mirror, make contact with your eyes and recite your four items from above. This is called mirror work.

If you don't have time, the truth is, you don't have priorities. Think harder; don't work harder.
~Tim Ferris~

Loving Mind

I am worthy of love because _____

_____

I accept all of me with love, including _____

_____

I deserve to be happy because _____

_____

TODAY'S DATE: ___/___/___

Grateful Spirit

List one person, one item (tangible or nontangible), and one personal attribute you are grateful for and why.

1) _____
   _____

2) _____
   _____

3) _____
   _____

Healthy Body

Being healthy is about showing love and respect for your body. Write your main health goal and one action you will do today to work towards that goal.

My main health goal is _____
_____

My action item today is _____
_____

Positive Outlook

What are three things you want at some point in your life? (Big, small, or in between.)

1) _____
2) _____
3) _____

Great potential lies in the person doing the job not in the job itself.

TODAY'S DATE: ___ / ___ / ___

Centered Breath

*First, **center your body** by sitting still, closing your eyes and breathing slowly and deeply for 15 breaths. Your lower ribs should expand with each inhale and contract with each exhale.*

My daily mantra is _____
_____

Today I love myself for _____
_____

Today I forgive myself for _____
_____

Today I promise myself that _____
_____

Looking in a mirror, make contact with your eyes and recite your four items from above. This is called mirror work.

Respect is a sign of love and acceptance, both for yourself and for others. Today, think about ways to show more respect for yourself and choose one to start doing right away.

Loving Mind

I am worthy of love because _____
_____

I accept all of me with love, including _____
_____

I deserve to be happy because _____
_____

TODAY'S DATE: /   /

Grateful Spirit

List one person, one item (tangible or nontangible), and one personal attribute you are grateful for and why.

1) _____

_____

2) _____

_____

3) _____

_____

Healthy Body

Being healthy is about showing love and respect for your body. Write your main health goal and one action you will do today to work towards that goal.

My main health goal is _____

_____

My action item today is _____

_____

Positive Outlook

What are three things you want at some point in your life? (Big, small, or in between.)

1) _____
2) _____
3) _____

Show respect to others, if for no other reason than they are human too.

TODAY'S DATE: ____ / ____ / ____

Centered Breath

*First, **center your body** by sitting still, closing your eyes and breathing slowly and deeply for 15 breaths. Your lower ribs should expand with each inhale and contract with each exhale.*

My daily mantra is _____
_____

Today I love myself for _____
_____

Today I forgive myself for _____
_____

Today I promise myself that _____
_____

Looking in a mirror, make contact with your eyes and recite your four items from above. This is called mirror work.

Great relationships are not without problems.
They become great because both are willing to understand mistakes, forgive each other, and find a way to make it work.

Loving Mind

I am worthy of love because _____
_____

I accept all of me with love, including _____
_____

I deserve to be happy because _____
_____

TODAY'S DATE: ____ / ____ / ____

Grateful Spirit

List one person, one item (tangible or nontangible), and one personal attribute you are grateful for and why.

1) _____

_____

2) _____

_____

3) _____

_____

Healthy Body

Being healthy is about showing love and respect for your body. Write your main health goal and one action you will do today to work towards that goal.

My main health goal is _____

_____

My action item today is _____

_____

Positive Outlook

What are three things you want at some point in your life? (Big, small, or in between.)

1) _____
2) _____
3) _____

One-sided relationships cannot last because they are out of balance.

TODAY'S DATE: /   /

Centered Breath

*First, **center your body** by sitting still, closing your eyes and breathing slowly and deeply for 15 breaths. Your lower ribs should expand with each inhale and contract with each exhale.*

My daily mantra is _____

_____

Today I love myself for _____

_____

Today I forgive myself for _____

_____

Today I promise myself that _____

_____

Looking in a mirror, make contact with your eyes and recite your four items from above. This is called mirror work.

Communication is only effective when we communicate in a way that is meaningful to the recipient, not ourselves.
~Rich Simmonds~

Loving Mind

I am worthy of love because _____

_____

I accept all of me with love, including _____

_____

I deserve to be happy because _____

_____

TODAY'S DATE: ___ / ___ / ___

Grateful Spirit

List one person, one item (tangible or nontangible), and one personal attribute you are grateful for and why.

1) _____
   _____

2) _____
   _____

3) _____
   _____

Healthy Body

Being healthy is about showing love and respect for your body. Write your main health goal and one action you will do today to work towards that goal.

My main health goal is _____
_____

My action item today is _____
_____

Positive Outlook

What are three things you want at some point in your life? (Big, small, or in between.)

1) _____
2) _____
3) _____

Understanding people improves our ability to communicate with others.

TODAY'S DATE: /   /

Centered Breath

*First, **center your body** by sitting still, closing your eyes and breathing slowly and deeply for 15 breaths. Your lower ribs should expand with each inhale and contract with each exhale.*

My daily mantra is _____
_____

Today I love myself for _____
_____

Today I forgive myself for _____
_____

Today I promise myself that _____
_____

Looking in a mirror, make contact with your eyes and recite your four items from above. This is called mirror work.

Success requires change. Change takes work. Being willing to work on yourself every day will take you down the path of lasting change and success - if you keep going.

Loving Mind

I am worthy of love because _____
_____

I accept all of me with love, including _____
_____

I deserve to be happy because _____
_____

TODAY'S DATE: /   /

Grateful Spirit

List one person, one item (tangible or nontangible), and one personal attribute you are grateful for and why.

1) _____

_____

2) _____

_____

3) _____

_____

Healthy Body

Being healthy is about showing love and respect for your body. Write your main health goal and one action you will do today to work towards that goal.

My main health goal is _____

_____

My action item today is _____

_____

Positive Outlook

What are three things you want at some point in your life? (Big, small, or in between.)

1) _____
2) _____
3) _____

Success in anything is never instantaneous.

TODAY'S DATE: ___ / ___ / ___

Centered Breath

*First, **center your body** by sitting still, closing your eyes and breathing slowly and deeply for 15 breaths. Your lower ribs should expand with each inhale and contract with each exhale.*

My daily mantra is _____
_____

Today I love myself for _____
_____

Today I forgive myself for _____
_____

Today I promise myself that _____
_____

Looking in a mirror, make contact with your eyes and recite your four items from above. This is called mirror work.

Giving frees us from the familiar territory of our own needs by opening our minds to...the needs of others.
~Barbara Bush~

Loving Mind

I am worthy of love because _____
_____

I accept all of me with love, including _____
_____

I deserve to be happy because _____
_____

TODAY'S DATE: ___ / ___ / ___

Grateful Spirit

List one person, one item (tangible or nontangible), and one personal attribute you are grateful for and why.

1) _____
   _____

2) _____
   _____

3) _____
   _____

Healthy Body

Being healthy is about showing love and respect for your body. Write your main health goal and one action you will do today to work towards that goal.

My main health goal is _____
_____

My action item today is _____
_____

Positive Outlook

What are three things you want at some point in your life? (Big, small, or in between.)

1) _____
2) _____
3) _____

Focus on what you are here to give and success will follow.

TODAY'S DATE: ___ / ___ / ___

Centered Breath

*First, **center your body** by sitting still, closing your eyes and breathing slowly and deeply for 15 breaths. Your lower ribs should expand with each inhale and contract with each exhale.*

My daily mantra is _____
_____

Today I love myself for _____
_____

Today I forgive myself for _____
_____

Today I promise myself that _____
_____

Looking in a mirror, make contact with your eyes and recite your four items from above. This is called mirror work.

You are uniquely you!
What are three talents you have?
Choose one to share with others today.

Loving Mind

I am worthy of love because _____
_____

I accept all of me with love, including _____
_____

I deserve to be happy because _____
_____

TODAY'S DATE: ___ / ___ / ___

Grateful Spirit

List one person, one item (tangible or nontangible), and one personal attribute you are grateful for and why.

1) _____

_____

2) _____

_____

3) _____

_____

Healthy Body

Being healthy is about showing love and respect for your body. Write your main health goal and one action you will do today to work towards that goal.

My main health goal is _____

_____

My action item today is _____

_____

Positive Outlook

What are three things you want at some point in your life? (Big, small, or in between.)

1) _____
2) _____
3) _____

You are special and unique.
There is only one you in the whole world.

TODAY'S DATE: /   /

Centered Breath

*First, **center your body** by sitting still, closing your eyes and breathing slowly and deeply for 15 breaths. Your lower ribs should expand with each inhale and contract with each exhale.*

My daily mantra is _____
_____

Today I love myself for _____
_____

Today I forgive myself for _____
_____

Today I promise myself that _____
_____

Looking in a mirror, make contact with your eyes and recite your four items from above. This is called mirror work.

In life, there will always be challenges. Do you have any challenges in your life right now? What are they? How can you look at your challenges as opportunities?

Loving Mind

I am worthy of love because _____
_____

I accept all of me with love, including _____
_____

I deserve to be happy because _____
_____

TODAY'S DATE: ___ / ___ / ___

Grateful Spirit

List one person, one item (tangible or nontangible), and one personal attribute you are grateful for and why.

1) _____
   _____

2) _____
   _____

3) _____
   _____

Healthy Body

Being healthy is about showing love and respect for your body. Write your main health goal and one action you will do today to work towards that goal.

My main health goal is _____
_____

My action item today is _____
_____

Positive Outlook

What are three things you want at some point in your life? (Big, small, or in between.)

1) _____
2) _____
3) _____

Be willing to see challenges as opportunities.

TODAY'S DATE: ___/___/___

Centered Breath

*First, **center your body** by sitting still, closing your eyes and breathing slowly and deeply for 15 breaths. Your lower ribs should expand with each inhale and contract with each exhale.*

My daily mantra is _____

_____

Today I love myself for _____

_____

Today I forgive myself for _____

_____

Today I promise myself that _____

_____

Looking in a mirror, make contact with your eyes and recite your four items from above. This is called mirror work.

You are lovable and worth loving.
Just because others may not have shown you the love you deserve in the past, does not make you any less lovable.

Loving Mind

I am worthy of love because _____

_____

I accept all of me with love, including _____

_____

I deserve to be happy because _____

_____

TODAY'S DATE: ___ / ___ / ___

Grateful Spirit

List one person, one item (tangible or nontangible), and one personal attribute you are grateful for and why.

1) _____

_____

2) _____

_____

3) _____

_____

Healthy Body

Being healthy is about showing love and respect for your body. Write your main health goal and one action you will do today to work towards that goal.

My main health goal is _____

_____

My action item today is _____

_____

Positive Outlook

What are three things you want at some point in your life? (Big, small, or in between.)

1) _____
2) _____
3) _____

Fall in love with yourself and, all of the sudden, you will love the world more.

TODAY'S DATE: ___ / ___ / ___

Centered Breath

*First, **center your body** by sitting still, closing your eyes and breathing slowly and deeply for 15 breaths. Your lower ribs should expand with each inhale and contract with each exhale.*

My daily mantra is _____
_____

Today I love myself for _____
_____

Today I forgive myself for _____
_____

Today I promise myself that _____
_____

Looking in a mirror, make contact with your eyes and recite your four items from above. This is called mirror work.

Feelings are energy and energy needs to be released. Expressing your feelings in healthy, positive ways will help you feel better and discover new things about your amazing self.

Loving Mind

I am worthy of love because _____
_____

I accept all of me with love, including _____
_____

I deserve to be happy because _____
_____

TODAY'S DATE: /   /

Grateful Spirit

List one person, one item (tangible or nontangible), and one personal attribute you are grateful for and why.

1) _____
_____

2) _____
_____

3) _____
_____

Healthy Body

Being healthy is about showing love and respect for your body. Write your main health goal and one action you will do today to work towards that goal.

My main health goal is _____
_____

My action item today is _____
_____

Positive Outlook

What are three things you want at some point in your life? (Big, small, or in between.)

1) _____
2) _____
3) _____

*Be willing to express yourself
in healthy, positive ways.*

TODAY'S DATE: /   /

Centered Breath

*First, **center your body** by sitting still, closing your eyes and breathing slowly and deeply for 15 breaths. Your lower ribs should expand with each inhale and contract with each exhale.*

My daily mantra is _____
_____

Today I love myself for _____
_____

Today I forgive myself for _____
_____

Today I promise myself that _____
_____

Looking in a mirror, make contact with your eyes and recite your four items from above. This is called mirror work.

Your opinion is important because you are important. Do not be afraid to respectfully express your opinion. It's okay if others don't agree with you. Love them anyway.

Loving Mind

I am worthy of love because _____
_____

I accept all of me with love, including _____
_____

I deserve to be happy because _____
_____

TODAY'S DATE: /   /

Grateful Spirit

List one person, one item (tangible or nontangible), and one personal attribute you are grateful for and why.

1) _____
_____

2) _____
_____

3) _____
_____

Healthy Body

Being healthy is about showing love and respect for your body. Write your main health goal and one action you will do today to work towards that goal.

My main health goal is _____
_____

My action item today is _____
_____

Positive Outlook

What are three things you want at some point in your life? (Big, small, or in between.)

1) _____
2) _____
3) _____

You are important and your opinion matters.

TODAY'S DATE: ___ / ___ / ___

Centered Breath

*First, **center your body** by sitting still, closing your eyes and breathing slowly and deeply for 15 breaths. Your lower ribs should expand with each inhale and contract with each exhale.*

My daily mantra is _____
_____

Today I love myself for _____
_____

Today I forgive myself for _____
_____

Today I promise myself that _____
_____

Looking in a mirror, make contact with your eyes and recite your four items from above. This is called mirror work.

*You have not lived today until you have done something
for someone who can never repay you.
~John Bunyan~*

Loving Mind

I am worthy of love because _____
_____

I accept all of me with love, including _____
_____

I deserve to be happy because _____
_____

TODAY'S DATE: ____ / ____ / ____

Grateful Spirit

List one person, one item (tangible or nontangible), and one personal attribute you are grateful for and why.

1) _____
   _____

2) _____
   _____

3) _____
   _____

Healthy Body

Being healthy is about showing love and respect for your body. Write your main health goal and one action you will do today to work towards that goal.

My main health goal is _____
_____

My action item today is _____
_____

Positive Outlook

What are three things you want at some point in your life? (Big, small, or in between.)

1) _____
2) _____
3) _____

Secure people find joy
in raising others up.

TODAY'S DATE: /   /

Centered Breath

*First, **center your body** by sitting still, closing your eyes and breathing slowly and deeply for 15 breaths. Your lower ribs should expand with each inhale and contract with each exhale.*

My daily mantra is _____
_____

Today I love myself for _____
_____

Today I forgive myself for _____
_____

Today I promise myself that _____
_____

Looking in a mirror, make contact with your eyes and recite your four items from above. This is called mirror work.

There is a Higher Power that wants only good things for you. When you feel anxious, close your eyes and say, "Everything works together for my highest and best good."

Loving Mind

I am worthy of love because _____
_____

I accept all of me with love, including _____
_____

I deserve to be happy because _____
_____

TODAY'S DATE: /   /

Grateful Spirit

List one person, one item (tangible or nontangible), and one personal attribute you are grateful for and why.

1) _____
_____

2) _____
_____

3) _____
_____

Healthy Body

Being healthy is about showing love and respect for your body. Write your main health goal and one action you will do today to work towards that goal.

My main health goal is _____
_____

My action item today is _____
_____

Positive Outlook

What are three things you want at some point in your life? (Big, small, or in between.)

1) _____
2) _____
3) _____

Everything is working together for your highest and best good.

TODAY'S DATE: /   /

Centered Breath

*First, **center your body** by sitting still, closing your eyes and breathing slowly and deeply for 15 breaths. Your lower ribs should expand with each inhale and contract with each exhale.*

My daily mantra is _____

_____

Today I love myself for _____

_____

Today I forgive myself for _____

_____

Today I promise myself that _____

_____

Looking in a mirror, make contact with your eyes and recite your four items from above. This is called mirror work.

This Earth is a gift you get to enjoy and care for every day. Take some time today to notice something beautiful and wonderful about where you live.

Loving Mind

I am worthy of love because _____

_____

I accept all of me with love, including _____

_____

I deserve to be happy because _____

_____

TODAY'S DATE: /   /

Grateful Spirit

List one person, one item (tangible or nontangible), and one personal attribute you are grateful for and why.

1) _____

_____

2) _____

_____

3) _____

_____

Healthy Body

Being healthy is about showing love and respect for your body. Write your main health goal and one action you will do today to work towards that goal.

My main health goal is _____

_____

My action item today is _____

_____

Positive Outlook

What are three things you want at some point in your life? (Big, small, or in between.)

1) _____
2) _____
3) _____

You live in a beautiful world full of joy and wonder.

TODAY'S DATE: /   /

Centered Breath

*First, **center your body** by sitting still, closing your eyes and breathing slowly and deeply for 15 breaths. Your lower ribs should expand with each inhale and contract with each exhale.*

My daily mantra is _____
_____

Today I love myself for _____
_____

Today I forgive myself for _____
_____

Today I promise myself that _____
_____

Looking in a mirror, make contact with your eyes and recite your four items from above. This is called mirror work.

Your brain is made to learn, and new things to learn surround you every day. You have the privilege of choosing from so many exciting topics. Pick one new thing to learn about today!

Loving Mind

I am worthy of love because _____
_____

I accept all of me with love, including _____
_____

I deserve to be happy because _____
_____

TODAY'S DATE: ___ / ___ / ___

Grateful Spirit

List one person, one item (tangible or nontangible), and one personal attribute you are grateful for and why.

1) _____
   _____

2) _____
   _____

3) _____
   _____

Healthy Body

Being healthy is about showing love and respect for your body. Write your main health goal and one action you will do today to work towards that goal.

My main health goal is _____
_____

My action item today is _____
_____

Positive Outlook

What are three things you want at some point in your life? (Big, small, or in between.)

1) _____
2) _____
3) _____

Start loving learning and be willing to learn new things.

TODAY'S DATE: /   /

Centered Breath

*First, **center your body** by sitting still, closing your eyes and breathing slowly and deeply for 15 breaths. Your lower ribs should expand with each inhale and contract with each exhale.*

My daily mantra is _____

_____

Today I love myself for _____

_____

Today I forgive myself for _____

_____

Today I promise myself that _____

_____

Looking in a mirror, make contact with your eyes and recite your four items from above. This is called mirror work.

You are perfectly you. You can do so many things. Love yourself for who you are. Today, close your eyes and feel how special you are; filling your heart with joy and gratitude for yourself.

Loving Mind

I am worthy of love because _____

_____

I accept all of me with love, including _____

_____

I deserve to be happy because _____

_____

TODAY'S DATE: ___ / ___ / ___

Grateful Spirit

List one person, one item (tangible or nontangible), and one personal attribute you are grateful for and why.

1) _____
   _____
2) _____
   _____
3) _____
   _____

Healthy Body

Being healthy is about showing love and respect for your body. Write your main health goal and one action you will do today to work towards that goal.

My main health goal is _____
_____

My action item today is _____
_____

Positive Outlook

What are three things you want at some point in your life? (Big, small, or in between.)

1) _____
2) _____
3) _____

Love and accept yourself
just the way you are.

TODAY'S DATE: ____ / ____ / ____

Centered Breath

*First, **center your body** by sitting still, closing your eyes and breathing slowly and deeply for 15 breaths. Your lower ribs should expand with each inhale and contract with each exhale.*

My daily mantra is _____
_____

Today I love myself for _____
_____

Today I forgive myself for _____
_____

Today I promise myself that _____
_____

Looking in a mirror, make contact with your eyes and recite your four items from above. This is called mirror work.

> You have within you right now, everything you need to deal with whatever the world can throw at you.
> ~Brian Tracy~

Loving Mind

I am worthy of love because _____
_____

I accept all of me with love, including _____
_____

I deserve to be happy because _____
_____

TODAY'S DATE: /   /

Grateful Spirit

List one person, one item (tangible or nontangible), and one personal attribute you are grateful for and why.

1) _____

_____

2) _____

_____

3) _____

_____

Healthy Body

Being healthy is about showing love and respect for your body. Write your main health goal and one action you will do today to work towards that goal.

My main health goal is _____

_____

My action item today is _____

_____

Positive Outlook

What are three things you want at some point in your life? (Big, small, or in between.)

1) _____
2) _____
3) _____

You are powerful.
All you need is within you.

TODAY'S DATE: /   /

Centered Breath

*First, **center your body** by sitting still, closing your eyes and breathing slowly and deeply for 15 breaths. Your lower ribs should expand with each inhale and contract with each exhale.*

My daily mantra is _____
_____

Today I love myself for _____
_____

Today I forgive myself for _____
_____

Today I promise myself that _____
_____

Looking in a mirror, make contact with your eyes and recite your four items from above. This is called mirror work.

You are the creator of your own, fantastic world.
Make it be whatever brings you joy.
Today, do something creative with someone you love.

Loving Mind

I am worthy of love because _____
_____

I accept all of me with love, including _____
_____

I deserve to be happy because _____
_____

TODAY'S DATE: /   /

Grateful Spirit

List one person, one item (tangible or nontangible), and one personal attribute you are grateful for and why.

1) _____
_____

2) _____
_____

3) _____
_____

Healthy Body

Being healthy is about showing love and respect for your body. Write your main health goal and one action you will do today to work towards that goal.

My main health goal is _____
_____

My action item today is _____
_____

Positive Outlook

What are three things you want at some point in your life? (Big, small, or in between.)

1) _____
2) _____
3) _____

You have amazing and creative ideas.

TODAY'S DATE: /   /

Centered Breath

First, **center your body** *by sitting still, closing your eyes and breathing slowly and deeply for 15 breaths. Your lower ribs should expand with each inhale and contract with each exhale.*

My daily mantra is _____

_____

Today I love myself for _____

_____

Today I forgive myself for _____

_____

Today I promise myself that _____

_____

Looking in a mirror, make contact with your eyes and recite your four items from above. This is called mirror work.

You are braver than you believe, stronger than you seem, and smarter than you think.
~Winnie the Pooh by A. A. Milne~

Loving Mind

I am worthy of love because _____

_____

I accept all of me with love, including _____

_____

I deserve to be happy because _____

_____

TODAY'S DATE: ___ / ___ / ___

Grateful Spirit

List one person, one item (tangible or nontangible), and one personal attribute you are grateful for and why.

1) _____
   _____

2) _____
   _____

3) _____
   _____

Healthy Body

Being healthy is about showing love and respect for your body. Write your main health goal and one action you will do today to work towards that goal.

My main health goal is _____
_____

My action item today is _____
_____

Positive Outlook

What are three things you want at some point in your life? (Big, small, or in between.)

1) _____
2) _____
3) _____

*You have so much power inside you.
Believe in yourself and always keep trying.*

TODAY'S DATE: /   /

Centered Breath

*First, **center your body** by sitting still, closing your eyes and breathing slowly and deeply for 15 breaths. Your lower ribs should expand with each inhale and contract with each exhale.*

My daily mantra is _____

_____

Today I love myself for _____

_____

Today I forgive myself for _____

_____

Today I promise myself that _____

_____

Looking in a mirror, make contact with your eyes and recite your four items from above. This is called mirror work.

Reconnect with nature today. Go outside and stand barefoot in grass, or silently watch a sunrise or sunset. There is peace and healing in nature.

Loving Mind

I am worthy of love because _____

_____

I accept all of me with love, including _____

_____

I deserve to be happy because _____

_____

TODAY'S DATE: ___ / ___ / ___

Grateful Spirit

List one person, one item (tangible or nontangible), and one personal attribute you are grateful for and why.

1) _____
   _____

2) _____
   _____

3) _____
   _____

Healthy Body

Being healthy is about showing love and respect for your body. Write your main health goal and one action you will do today to work towards that goal.

My main health goal is _____
_____

My action item today is _____
_____

Positive Outlook

What are three things you want at some point in your life? (Big, small, or in between.)

1) _____
2) _____
3) _____

*Go into nature to feed your soul,
to lift you up and make you whole.*

TODAY'S DATE: ____ / ____ / ____

Centered Breath

*First, **center your body** by sitting still, closing your eyes and breathing slowly and deeply for 15 breaths. Your lower ribs should expand with each inhale and contract with each exhale.*

My daily mantra is _____
_____

Today I love myself for _____
_____

Today I forgive myself for _____
_____

Today I promise myself that _____
_____

Looking in a mirror, make contact with your eyes and recite your four items from above. This is called mirror work.

A dream may be a wish, but wishes rarely come true without action. Write down your wish and turn it into an actionable goal.

Loving Mind

I am worthy of love because _____
_____

I accept all of me with love, including _____
_____

I deserve to be happy because _____
_____

TODAY'S DATE: ___ / ___ / ___

Grateful Spirit

List one person, one item (tangible or nontangible), and one personal attribute you are grateful for and why.

1) _____
   _____

2) _____
   _____

3) _____
   _____

Healthy Body

Being healthy is about showing love and respect for your body. Write your main health goal and one action you will do today to work towards that goal.

My main health goal is _____
_____

My action item today is _____
_____

Positive Outlook

What are three things you want at some point in your life? (Big, small, or in between.)

1) _____
2) _____
3) _____

Keep dreaming, but stop wishing.
Dreams come true through working your goals.

TODAY'S DATE: /   /

Centered Breath

*First, **center your body** by sitting still, closing your eyes and breathing slowly and deeply for 15 breaths. Your lower ribs should expand with each inhale and contract with each exhale.*

My daily mantra is _____
_____

Today I love myself for _____
_____

Today I forgive myself for _____
_____

Today I promise myself that _____
_____

Looking in a mirror, make contact with your eyes and recite your four items from above. This is called mirror work.

Change happens every day.
Focus your energy on building the new instead of resisting the old and you open yourself to possibility.

Loving Mind

I am worthy of love because _____
_____

I accept all of me with love, including _____
_____

I deserve to be happy because _____
_____

TODAY'S DATE: ___ / ___ / ___

Grateful Spirit

List one person, one item (tangible or nontangible), and one personal attribute you are grateful for and why.

1) _____
   _____

2) _____
   _____

3) _____
   _____

Healthy Body

Being healthy is about showing love and respect for your body. Write your main health goal and one action you will do today to work towards that goal.

My main health goal is _____
_____

My action item today is _____
_____

Positive Outlook

What are three things you want at some point in your life? (Big, small, or in between.)

1) _____
2) _____
3) _____

What you are resisting will keep persisting.

TODAY'S DATE: /   /

Centered Breath

*First, **center your body** by sitting still, closing your eyes and breathing slowly and deeply for 15 breaths. Your lower ribs should expand with each inhale and contract with each exhale.*

My daily mantra is _____

_____

Today I love myself for _____

_____

Today I forgive myself for _____

_____

Today I promise myself that _____

_____

Looking in a mirror, make contact with your eyes and recite your four items from above. This is called mirror work.

No matter how many mistakes you make or how slow you progress, you are still way ahead of everyone who isn't trying.
~Tony Robbins~

Loving Mind

I am worthy of love because _____

_____

I accept all of me with love, including _____

_____

I deserve to be happy because _____

_____

TODAY'S DATE: ___ / ___ / ___

Grateful Spirit

List one person, one item (tangible or nontangible), and one personal attribute you are grateful for and why.

1) _____

_____

2) _____

_____

3) _____

_____

Healthy Body

Being healthy is about showing love and respect for your body. Write your main health goal and one action you will do today to work towards that goal.

My main health goal is _____

_____

My action item today is _____

_____

Positive Outlook

What are three things you want at some point in your life? (Big, small, or in between.)

1) _____
2) _____
3) _____

Just start, and you've already done the hardest part.

TODAY'S DATE: /   /

Centered Breath

*First, **center your body** by sitting still, closing your eyes and breathing slowly and deeply for 15 breaths. Your lower ribs should expand with each inhale and contract with each exhale.*

My daily mantra is _____
_____

Today I love myself for _____
_____

Today I forgive myself for _____
_____

Today I promise myself that _____
_____

Looking in a mirror, make contact with your eyes and recite your four items from above. This is called mirror work.

*The meditation mantra **So Hum** means "I am that." You are one with all of life and all of life is one with you. What you do to others you do to yourself.*

Loving Mind

I am worthy of love because _____
_____

I accept all of me with love, including _____
_____

I deserve to be happy because _____
_____

TODAY'S DATE: ____ / ____ / ____

Grateful Spirit

List one person, one item (tangible or nontangible), and one personal attribute you are grateful for and why.

1) _____

_____

2) _____

_____

3) _____

_____

Healthy Body

Being healthy is about showing love and respect for your body. Write your main health goal and one action you will do today to work towards that goal.

My main health goal is _____

_____

My action item today is _____

_____

Positive Outlook

What are three things you want at some point in your life? (Big, small, or in between.)

1) _____
2) _____
3) _____

Breathing in (So), I give love to myself.
Breathing out (Hum), I send love to others.

TODAY'S DATE   /   /

Centered Breath

*First, **center your body** by sitting still, closing your eyes and breathing slowly and deeply for 15 breaths. Your lower ribs should expand with each inhale and contract with each exhale.*

My daily mantra is _____
_____

Today I love myself for _____
_____

Today I forgive myself for _____
_____

Today I promise myself that _____
_____

Looking in a mirror, make contact with your eyes and recite your four items from above. This is called mirror work.

Today, write a letter of forgiveness to someone who has hurt you. You don't need to send the letter, just write it. You can burn the letter, releasing negative emotions as it disappears.

Loving Mind

I am worthy of love because _____
_____

I accept all of me with love, including _____
_____

I deserve to be happy because _____
_____

TODAY'S DATE: /   /

Grateful Spirit

List one person, one item (tangible or nontangible), and one personal attribute you are grateful for and why.

1) _____
   _____

2) _____
   _____

3) _____
   _____

Healthy Body

Being healthy is about showing love and respect for your body. Write your main health goal and one action you will do today to work towards that goal.

My main health goal is _____
_____

My action item today is _____
_____

Positive Outlook

What are three things you want at some point in your life? (Big, small, or in between.)

1) _____
2) _____
3) _____

*Don't drink the poison of grudge-holding.
Detox your life by releasing anger towards others.*

TODAY'S DATE: /   /

Centered Breath

*First, **center your body** by sitting still, closing your eyes and breathing slowly and deeply for 15 breaths. Your lower ribs should expand with each inhale and contract with each exhale.*

My daily mantra is _____

_____

Today I love myself for _____

_____

Today I forgive myself for _____

_____

Today I promise myself that _____

_____

Looking in a mirror, make contact with your eyes and recite your four items from above. This is called mirror work.

Vulnerability is not winning or losing. It's having the courage to show up when you can't control the outcome.
~Brené Brown~

Loving Mind

I am worthy of love because _____

_____

I accept all of me with love, including _____

_____

I deserve to be happy because _____

_____

TODAY'S DATE: ___ / ___ / ___

Grateful Spirit

List one person, one item (tangible or nontangible), and one personal attribute you are grateful for and why.

1) _____

_____

2) _____

_____

3) _____

_____

Healthy Body

Being healthy is about showing love and respect for your body. Write your main health goal and one action you will do today to work towards that goal.

My main health goal is _____

_____

My action item today is _____

_____

Positive Outlook

What are three things you want at some point in your life? (Big, small, or in between.)

1) _____
2) _____
3) _____

Be you.
The people who don't like it aren't worth your energy.

TODAY'S DATE: /   /

Centered Breath

*First, **center your body** by sitting still, closing your eyes and breathing slowly and deeply for 15 breaths. Your lower ribs should expand with each inhale and contract with each exhale.*

My daily mantra is _____
_____

Today I love myself for _____
_____

Today I forgive myself for _____
_____

Today I promise myself that _____
_____

Looking in a mirror, make contact with your eyes and recite your four items from above. This is called mirror work.

Five to Survive: Identify FIVE things that relieve your stress. Your list can include: exercise, meditation, hiking, family, etc. You will use at least one of these every day to reduce stress.

Loving Mind

I am worthy of love because _____
_____

I accept all of me with love, including _____
_____

I deserve to be happy because _____
_____

TODAY'S DATE: ____ / ____ / ____

Grateful Spirit

List one person, one item (tangible or nontangible), and one personal attribute you are grateful for and why.

1) _____

_____

2) _____

_____

3) _____

_____

Healthy Body

Being healthy is about showing love and respect for your body. Write your main health goal and one action you will do today to work towards that goal.

My main health goal is _____

_____

My action item today is _____

_____

Positive Outlook

What are three things you want at some point in your life? (Big, small, or in between.)

1) _____
2) _____
3) _____

Don't fail to plan or you're planning to fail.

TODAY'S DATE: /   /

Centered Breath

*First, **center your body** by sitting still, closing your eyes and breathing slowly and deeply for 15 breaths. Your lower ribs should expand with each inhale and contract with each exhale.*

My daily mantra is _____

_____

Today I love myself for _____

_____

Today I forgive myself for _____

_____

Today I promise myself that _____

_____

Looking in a mirror, make contact with your eyes and recite your four items from above. This is called mirror work.

Authenticity is being true to your morals, values, and personality in an honest and responsible way, despite the pressures around you to fit in.

Loving Mind

I am worthy of love because _____

_____

I accept all of me with love, including _____

_____

I deserve to be happy because _____

_____

TODAY'S DATE: ____ / ____ / ____

Grateful Spirit

List one person, one item (tangible or nontangible), and one personal attribute you are grateful for and why.

1) _____
_____

2) _____
_____

3) _____
_____

Healthy Body

Being healthy is about showing love and respect for your body. Write your main health goal and one action you will do today to work towards that goal.

My main health goal is _____
_____

My action item today is _____
_____

Positive Outlook

What are three things you want at some point in your life? (Big, small, or in between.)

1) _____
2) _____
3) _____

Being your authentic self inspires others.

TODAY'S DATE: /   /

Centered Breath

*First, **center your body** by sitting still, closing your eyes and breathing slowly and deeply for 15 breaths. Your lower ribs should expand with each inhale and contract with each exhale.*

My daily mantra is _____

_____

Today I love myself for _____

_____

Today I forgive myself for _____

_____

Today I promise myself that _____

_____

Looking in a mirror, make contact with your eyes and recite your four items from above. This is called mirror work.

Think about the **abundance** in your life.
Today, make a list of the abundance around you.
Share your list with a friend or loved one.

Loving Mind

I am worthy of love because _____

_____

I accept all of me with love, including _____

_____

I deserve to be happy because _____

_____

TODAY'S DATE: /   /

Grateful Spirit

List one person, one item (tangible or nontangible), and one personal attribute you are grateful for and why.

1) _____

_____

2) _____

_____

3) _____

_____

Healthy Body

Being healthy is about showing love and respect for your body. Write your main health goal and one action you will do today to work towards that goal.

My main health goal is _____

_____

My action item today is _____

_____

Positive Outlook

What are three things you want at some point in your life? (Big, small, or in between.)

1) _____
2) _____
3) _____

Gratitude puts us in tune with the energy of abundance.

TODAY'S DATE: ___ / ___ / ___

Centered Breath

*First, **center your body** by sitting still, closing your eyes and breathing slowly and deeply for 15 breaths. Your lower ribs should expand with each inhale and contract with each exhale.*

My daily mantra is _____
_____

Today I love myself for _____
_____

Today I forgive myself for _____
_____

Today I promise myself that _____
_____

Looking in a mirror, make contact with your eyes and recite your four items from above. This is called mirror work.

*What you think you deserve
is what you're getting in life.
~Roxana Jones~*

Loving Mind

I am worthy of love because _____
_____

I accept all of me with love, including _____
_____

I deserve to be happy because _____
_____

TODAY'S DATE: ___ / ___ / ___

Grateful Spirit

List one person, one item (tangible or nontangible), and one personal attribute you are grateful for and why.

1) _____

_____

2) _____

_____

3) _____

_____

Healthy Body

Being healthy is about showing love and respect for your body. Write your main health goal and one action you will do today to work towards that goal.

My main health goal is _____

_____

My action item today is _____

_____

Positive Outlook

What are three things you want at some point in your life? (Big, small, or in between.)

1) _____
2) _____
3) _____

You deserve great things in your life.

TODAY'S DATE: ___/___/___

Centered Breath

*First, **center your body** by sitting still, closing your eyes and breathing slowly and deeply for 15 breaths. Your lower ribs should expand with each inhale and contract with each exhale.*

My daily mantra is _____

_____

Today I love myself for _____

_____

Today I forgive myself for _____

_____

Today I promise myself that _____

_____

Looking in a mirror, make contact with your eyes and recite your four items from above. This is called mirror work.

Your emotions are teachers.
Today, take ten minutes to sit quietly and "listen" to what your emotions are saying. Don't judge or fight it; accept and learn.

Loving Mind

I am worthy of love because _____

_____

I accept all of me with love, including _____

_____

I deserve to be happy because _____

_____

TODAY'S DATE: ___ / ___ / ___

Grateful Spirit

List one person, one item (tangible or nontangible), and one personal attribute you are grateful for and why.

1) _____
_____

2) _____
_____

3) _____
_____

Healthy Body

Being healthy is about showing love and respect for your body. Write your main health goal and one action you will do today to work towards that goal.

My main health goal is _____
_____

My action item today is _____
_____

Positive Outlook

What are three things you want at some point in your life? (Big, small, or in between.)

1) _____
2) _____
3) _____

Be willing to feel your emotions and accept what they are teaching you.

TODAY'S DATE: /   /

Centered Breath

*First, **center your body** by sitting still, closing your eyes and breathing slowly and deeply for 15 breaths. Your lower ribs should expand with each inhale and contract with each exhale.*

My daily mantra is _____

_____

Today I love myself for _____

_____

Today I forgive myself for _____

_____

Today I promise myself that _____

_____

Looking in a mirror, make contact with your eyes and recite your four items from above. This is called mirror work.

Never be ashamed of your feelings. Every feeling is important. Feelings are a way for us to understand ourselves and how we relate to the world and the people around us.

Loving Mind

I am worthy of love because _____

_____

I accept all of me with love, including _____

_____

I deserve to be happy because _____

_____

TODAY'S DATE: ___ / ___ / ___

Grateful Spirit

List one person, one item (tangible or nontangible), and one personal attribute you are grateful for and why.

1) _____
   _____

2) _____
   _____

3) _____
   _____

Healthy Body

Being healthy is about showing love and respect for your body. Write your main health goal and one action you will do today to work towards that goal.

My main health goal is _____
_____

My action item today is _____
_____

Positive Outlook

What are three things you want at some point in your life? (Big, small, or in between.)

1) _____
2) _____
3) _____

Your feelings and emotions are valid.

TODAY'S DATE: /   /

Centered Breath

*First, **center your body** by sitting still, closing your eyes and breathing slowly and deeply for 15 breaths. Your lower ribs should expand with each inhale and contract with each exhale.*

My daily mantra is _____
_____

Today I love myself for _____
_____

Today I forgive myself for _____
_____

Today I promise myself that _____
_____

Looking in a mirror, make contact with your eyes and recite your four items from above. This is called mirror work.

Often, we don't like things we don't understand or are new to us because they scare us. When you learn to move past the fear, there are so many things to enjoy about life.

Loving Mind

I am worthy of love because _____
_____

I accept all of me with love, including _____
_____

I deserve to be happy because _____
_____

TODAY'S DATE: ___ / ___ / ___

Grateful Spirit

List one person, one item (tangible or nontangible), and one personal attribute you are grateful for and why.

1) _____

_____

2) _____

_____

3) _____

_____

Healthy Body

Being healthy is about showing love and respect for your body. Write your main health goal and one action you will do today to work towards that goal.

My main health goal is _____

_____

My action item today is _____

_____

Positive Outlook

What are three things you want at some point in your life? (Big, small, or in between.)

1) _____
2) _____
3) _____

Be willing to let go of fear and doubt, and try new things.

You Did It!

Congratulations! You finished!

How do you feel?

Keep your momentum going by getting another *My High Five Journal* or try a new journal out. There's really no wrong way to keep going, just as long as you don't stop moving forward!

Need suggestions? Just ask me!

I have other journals or can suggest other journals (and amazing books) to help keep you on the path to becoming the **BEST VERSION OF YOU!**

Reach out anytime and I'm happy to help...

@faithjoybooks

www.faithjoybooks.com

www.ingramcontent.com/pod-product-compliance
Lightning Source LLC
Chambersburg PA
CBHW070101120526
44589CB00033B/1368